T0044804

# Adverbs Say "FINALLY!"

by Michael Dahl

illustrated by Maira Chiodi

PICTURE WINDOW BOOKS
a capstone imprint

Hello!
We're verbs.
Not ADVERBS.
Verbs. There's a
difference.

Right. You were probably expecting adverbs.
Adverbs *are* in the title of this book.
Adverbs Say FINALLY!

Verbs and adverbs go well together. Like peanut butter and jelly.
Or milk and cookies. Ooh! Or chicken and waffles!
Verbs don't mind being alone. But they have more fun when adverbs are around.
Let's let the adverbs tell their story . . .

Verbs are parts of speech that usually tell us something happened. Adverbs tell us *how* something happened.

"See" and "climb" are the verbs. Adverbs tell us *how* we see and *how* we climb—clearly, quickly, and so slowly!

Adverbs can describe how we do things.

Hooray! I made it! I dance happily!
I stand proudly.
And I'm going to lie down immediately.

OK, now we can say hello. Hi, readers! We're adverbs!
"High" is right. Too high. Way too high.
You said that weakly.
I say it "weekly" because it takes me a *week* to climb that ladder!

No, you said it weakly. Without energy.
And that, friends, is what adverbs do. We describe how things are done!

Adverbs can describe how we say something.

Excuse us.
Or you can say something politely.

Adverbs can describe physical actions.
They tell us how we move.

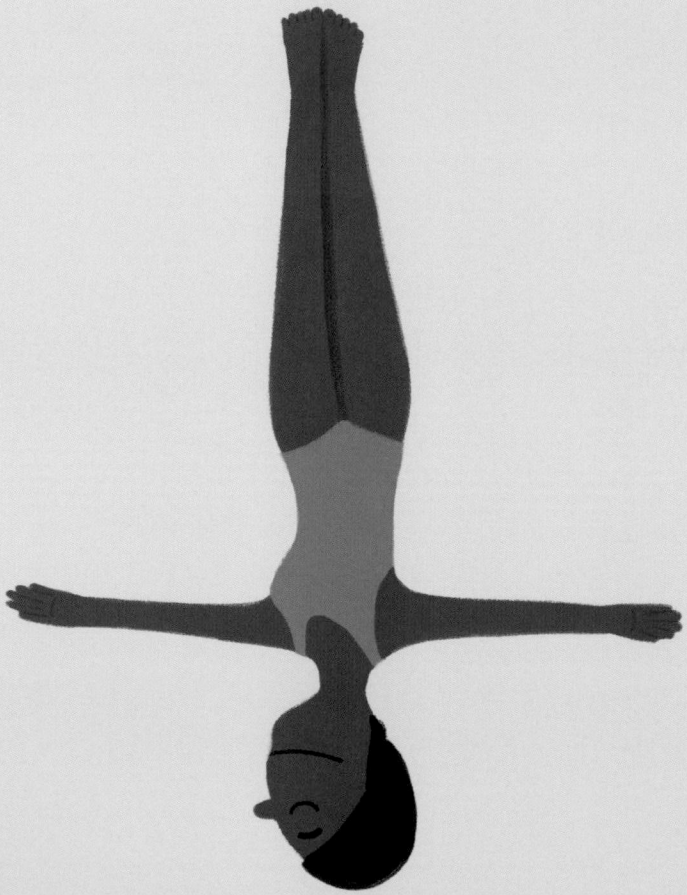

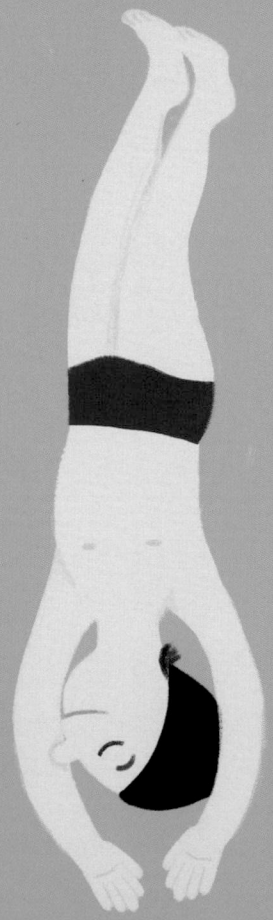

Ooh! She dives **fiercely**!

He dives **poorly** but **stylishly**!

Some adverbs tell us how often something is done.

I used to swim regularly.
That guest always gets a sunburn!
I rarely sit in the shade. I should put on sunblock soon.

Most adverbs aren't content to lie around.
They like to be where the action is.

Adverbs can be at the front, middle, or end of a sentence.

You can spot many adverbs by their ending.

Look! Most of those adverbs end in "ly."
This race is definitely giving me goosebumps!
The band plays noisily.
Honestly? I am having a great time.
LY
LY

Some adverbs tell us when something takes place.

I ate breakfast, and then I rushed over.
I arrived before they did.
I arrived yesterday!

Adverbs can also help adjectives describe things better.

The pink words are adjectives. They describe the cyclists and their bikes. The blue adverbs give us even more detail.
FINISH
Hooray! Orange won!!!

Adverbs make sentences more interesting.

And so the adverb sat there **silently** . . . **thoroughly** wet . . . and **miserably** cold.

# ALL ABOUT AMAZING ADVERBS

Adverbs are words that describe or modify verbs, adjectives, or even other adverbs.

I ran QUICKLY through the dark forest. (modifies the verb "ran"; *How did I run?*)
I dropped my VERY shiny penny into the wishing well. (modifies the adjective "shiny"; *How shiny?*)
The giant yelled SO LOUDLY! (the adverb "so" modifies the adverb "loudly"; *How loudly?*)

Adverbs can tell us *how* something is done.

The baby giraffe walked AWKWARDLY.
The tree fell NOISILY to the ground.

Adverbs can tell us *when* something happens.

I rode the school bus YESTERDAY.
She will climb the volcano TOMORROW.
They woke up EARLY to catch some worms.

Some adverbs tell us *how often* something happens.

He NEVER shares his chocolate treats with me.
SOMETIMES it snows in April.

Many adverbs end in the letters "ly."

The following words are adverbs that commonly modify other adverbs: "almost," "always," "definitely," "really," "so," "too," and "very."

## ABOUT THE AUTHOR

**Michael Dahl** is the author of more than 200 books for children and has won the AEP Distinguished Achievement Award three times for his nonfiction. He is the author of the bestselling *Bedtime for Batman* and *You're a Star, Wonder Woman!* picture books. He has written dozens of books of jokes, riddles, and puns. He likes to play with words. In grade school, he read the dictionary for fun. Really. Michael is proud to say that he has always been a noun. A PROPER noun, at that.

## ABOUT THE ILLUSTRATOR

**Maira Chiodi's** colorful, joyful work has appeared in magazines, books, games, and a variety of other products. As a child in Brazil, Maira spent hours cutting paper, painting, and reading—creating wildly imaginative worlds all her own. Today she feels lucky to be able to create and share her illustrations and designs with kids and grown-ups around the world. She divides her time between Canada and Brazil, finding inspiration for her art in nature, animation, and the culture of her native country.

## GLOSSARY

**action**—the act of doing something

**adjective**—a word that tells more about a noun or pronoun

**adverb**—a word that describes or modifies a verb, an adjective, or another adverb

**describe**—to tell about something

**modify**—to change or provide further detail about something

**physical**—having to do with something that can be seen and touched

**verb**—a word that shows an action or state of being (how something is, was, or will be)

## THINK ABOUT IT

1. What adverbs could you use to describe how a songbird sings? (Hint: Think about words ending in "ly.")
2. What adverbs could you use to describe how a racehorse runs?
3. What adverbs could you use to modify the adjectives in this sentence? The _____ small mouse fought the _____ big lion. Give at least three examples for each blank.

## READ MORE


**Heinrichs, Ann.** *Adverbs.* Language Rules. New York: AV2 by Weigl, 2018.

**Loewen, Nancy.** *The Big Problem (and the Squirrel Who Eventually Solved It): Understanding Adjectives and Adverbs.* Language on the Loose. North Mankato, MN: Picture Window Books, a Capstone imprint, 2016.

**Riggs, Kate.** *Adverbs.* Grammar Basics. Mankato, MN: Creative Education, 2013.


## INTERNET SITES

*Enchanted Learning: Grammar: Adverb*
https://www.enchantedlearning.com/grammar/partsofspeech/adverbs/index.shtml

*Grammaropolis: The Adverbs*
https://www.grammaropolis.com/adverb.php

*Schoolhouse Rock: Adverbs*
https://www.youtube.com/watch?v=dDwXHTcodNg

## LOOK FOR ALL THE PARTS OF SPEECH TITLES

# INDEX

adjectives, 24, 25, 28
adverb endings, 20, 21, 28
how often things happen, 16, 28
how things happen, 6, 7, 8, 11, 12, 14, 28
placement, 19
verbs, 2, 4, 6, 7, 28
when things happen, 22, 28

Editor: Jill Kalz
Designer: Lori Bye
Production Specialist: Katy LaVigne
The illustrations in this book were created digitally.

Picture Window Books are published by Capstone
1710 Roe Crest Drive, North Mankato, Minnesota 56003
www.capstonepub.com

Copyright © 2020 by Picture Window Books, a Capstone imprint. All rights reserved. No part of this publication may be reproduced in whole or in part, or stored in a retrieval system, or transmitted in any form or by any means, electronic, mechanical, photocopying, recording, or otherwise, without written permission of the publisher.

Library of Congress Cataloging-in-Publication Data is available on the Library of Congress website.
ISBN 978-1-5158-3872-2 (library binding)
ISBN 978-1-5158-4061-9 (paperback)
ISBN 978-1-5158-3877-7 (eBook PDF)
Summary: Whether diving from a very tall platform or crossing the finish line after a really grueling bike race, the adverbs have the perfect word: *finally*! Honestly, isn't it time for a quirky parts-of-speech adventure that subtly teaches grammar basics while readers are busy cheering loudly and giggling often?

All internet sites appearing in back matter were available and accurate when this book was sent to press.

Printed and bound in China.
001654